Walk In The Light
Of Darkness

Walk In The Light Of Darkness

A NOVEL

Betty White

2002

Walk In The Light
Of Darkness

This Book Is Dedicated To The Memory Of
Father Joseph Maher
And To People Everywhere Who Fight The Good Fight,
With Love, Gratitude And Deep Respect.
— Betty White

Preface

This remarkable story will inspire, comfort, confront and challenge you. You will find yourself walking as a sojourner with a man thrown into an unexpected darkness when his eyesight is suddenly gone, faith shattered and his soul cries out in anger, loneliness, and fear. The reader will feel the agony of a man who prayed for a new pair of eyes in order that he might continue the mission of Christ.

Father Joe's ministry—marked by kindness, faithfulness, simplicity and humility—became an inspiration for the myriad of persons within several parishes of South Carolina. As their underShepherd, he celebrated the daily tasks set before him, pouring out the Lord's blessing upon them all.

Three years ago, Agnes Eassy introduced me to Betty White while sharing with a grief support group. She tells me her story, then lets me read the manuscript of Journey into Darkness. I am touched by the honest, transparent way Betty writes. She becomes Joe's 'ministering angel' of mercy, and helps him see a greater light through the dreadful experience of blindness. Later, I met with Bishop Robert Baker and Monsignor James Carter of the Charleston Diocese who gave their encouragement. Betty's intense desire to remember the life and works of Father Joe and to acknowledge the testimony of those profoundly touched by his life, prompted me to assist in moving from written script to a published work and distribution.

This story reveals in an uncommon way the paradoxes of the human condition—the journey into darkness and light, fear contesting faith, and the evidence of the Lord's in mist of the uncertainty and confusion of His followers. This story unmasks the pretensions of a faith that promises the absence of pain and suffering, of a hope that assures and guarantees in all circumstances complete healing, of a love that embraces the grace of His unconditional love but avoids the truth of our weakness and sin.

At least these lessons: human condition is filled with suffering and pain; faith will be tested; we must never walk away from other's pain because of a feeling of inadequacy; we often cannot deal with their suffering if we cannot face our own mortality. Father Joe's story connects to our own wonderings of the mystery of pain and suffering and of the miracle of grace when walking through the shadowlands of suffering. This is a story of severe mercy and sovereign grace.

While one may read the story with full empathy compassion, another may lay it down and go about life, untouched and unchanged. For some, this small book will become a mirror to personal pain and loss. For others, Joe's story may serve as an asterisk to life, referring to a footnote of their journey into the foreboding, fearsome darkness of an emotional, physical or spiritual pain. Nevertheless, questions of the human condition remain. Where is God when we suffer? Is suffering retributive or redemptive? How shall we respond to another's suffering? How can we live well, die well, in the midst of suffering?

The journey toward the light continues. The grace of the sovereign and sufficient Christ remains.

Don C. Berry, Ph.D.
President, Institute of Religion and Health
Charleston, South Carolina

Author's Note

Father Joe never failed to mention the many fine people who did their best to help unlock the shackles of his blindness. Following is a special note that I think Father Joe would want me to include, thanking God for the good people in his life.

He was indebted in so many ways to his friend and physician, Dr. James Hayes and his wife, Barbara Hayes, Reverend Charles Day and Reverend Ernest Kennedy. To Sister Noreen Buttimer, Philip and Genevieve Noe. His friends Frances Frizelle and family. His "adopted family", Frank and Betty White, Gary and Debra White, Barbara and Charlie Thompson, Gary, Holly and Regan White. His housekeeper, Melonie Pinckney.

He was grateful to the "Tuesday morning walkers," Frances Frizelle, Mary and Joe Soffera.

His drivers who made sure he was able to visit the parish shut-ins. Inez Germroth, Jim Anderson, Mary Dickmann, Delores Wrenn, and Kay Reynolds.

To those faithful and special people who invited him into their homes for meals every few weeks on a regular basis: Bill Moore and his wife Anne. Dorie and Paul Neubegal. Jackie O'Shaughnessy. Mary and Joe Soffera and Deloris Soffera. Pauline and Bob Bissey and family. Frances and Bill Regan.

His friends in Georgetown, Jean Urtz, Beverly Turbeville, Barbara Dumm and others.

The children of Nativity School, staff members and

parishioners, his friends at the Elks Club, South Carolina Irish Historical Society, and Knights Of Columbus.

I would personally like to thank my husband Frank for all the love and kindness shown to Joe and his support of my efforts in writing this tribute. Also, I would like to thank my family and friends for their interest and encouragement. Special thanks to my "team" members Don, Agnes, Jo, and Holly.

Biography

Reverend Joseph Maher was born in Chicago on October 28, 1927, to Mary Margaret and James Maher, Irish immigrants from Killenaule, County Tipperary, Ireland. He was the oldest of five children. Joe grew up in a largely Polish area of Chicago. His father was employed at International Harvester and his mother stayed home with the children. He told stories of going to work in the laundry across from his home as a very young lad, picking up hangers, checking pockets (finders keepers), and cleaning floors. All of the Maher brothers worked in this laundry at one time or another.

Joe told stories of playing around the railroad tracks, taking coal to make small fires so he and his buddies could roast potatoes in the ground as they would "camp out" overnight in the backyard.

He also told of his great love of roller-skating and how he loved to go to the roller rink on Friday and Saturday nights wearing his boots with tassels, the fashion statement of the 40s for kids.

Two of his favorite tales had to do with skating. One day he came home to find his younger brother, wearing his boots and going out o to skate. Joe grabbed a dart from a game and threw it at his brother, driving it into the palm of his hand. "Needless to say," he joked, "there was a load of excitement in my house that day, and neither one of us was allowed to return to the rink for 2 weeks."

Another favorite story was the time around 15 years old when Joe made a date to meet a girl at the rink and promised to take her home on the bus that evening after skating. Unfortunately, she lived quite a distance away and Joe had to transfer from bus to bus several times causing him to arrive at home around midnight. Both parents were waiting up for him and once again there was excitement in the Maher home.

Following his graduation from Immaculate Heart Seminary in Compton, California, and Oscott College in Coldfield, England, he was ordained March 19, 1955, in London. He often spoke of the times when he and the other seminarians would ride their bikes along the English countryside. How they would ride to the local train station and take the train to London for the weekend. How he enjoyed playing the trombone in the school jazz band.

He did not want to serve as a priest in the Order in which he was ordained, so while at home in Chicago, looking into different options, a priest friend told him that the Bishop of the Diocese of Charleston, was in Ohio interviewing young priests for service in South Carolina. A phone call was made to the Bishop and an interview was set up for a few weeks later in Charleston. Joe arrived by train and was met by two diocesan priests who took him to the Bishop, and the rest is history.

He began his ministry in the diocese of Charleston in 1959 and served as either Pastor or Associate Pastor in the following parishes: St. Edwards, Murphy Village, Our Lady of the Rosary, Greenville; Blessed Sacrament, Charleston; St. Peter, Cheraw; Stella Maris, Sullivan's Island; St. Mary's, Georgetown; The Church of the Nativity, Charleston; Our Lady of Good Counsel, Folly Beach; St. James, Ritter; and St. Anthony, Walterboro.

Everywhere Joe served, he left a multitude of friends and

admirers, both catholic and non-catholic, and the stories of his devotion to his parishioners are legion.

At the time of his death, he was a Vicar For Clergy in the Internal Forum,

the Chaplain of the South Carolina Irish Historical Society, Member of the Knights of Columbus Council 6250, and Elks Lodge 242, all located in Charleston, South Carolina.

Why I Wrote This Story

I began to write this story about Father Joe Maher's "Walk In The Light of Darkness" about two months after his death in September 1998. In the five years of his blindness, Father Maher grew from someone in the depths of depression to a man who found happiness in his new and different life. He slowly learned not to accept his blindness as an end to life, but as a challenge to go on living. After his death, I found myself overflowing with desire to share this wonderful man's story with others. Father Maher was and will always be my hero.

Since ancient times, man has preserved his heroes in song and story. I feel that Father Maher is a hero for the new millennium. Not because of what he did, but because of what he endured. He carried his cross every second of the last five years of his life. Father Maher was not by any means a saint, but he left behind a wonderful legacy of what we can do when we have the gifts of faith, hope, and charity.

I thank God every day for allowing me the privilege of holding Father Joe's hand as he "walked in the light of darkness."

I Am Blind

Medical University of South Carolina
October 1993

Can you see who is here this morning? the doctor asked.

Well, I can just make out the shadows of you, doctor, Father Maher replied.

Can you see what I am doing? the doctor continued his questions.

I think you are shaking your hand back and forth.

How many fingers am I holding up?

Let me see. . .I have to get the right light. I believe you have three fingers up.

Good. Now, how many?

Two.

How many? the doctor repeated.

I think three. I can't see your little finger.

Can you see anything in this book?

I think there is a number two in the colors.

Fine, can you see anything else?

No, doctor.

Father Maher, I must tell you this morning that you are now legally blind.

Blind! You mean I'll never see again?

I'm not saying that. There is a possibility that, due to the massive regimen of steroids, you may get some further vision. I cannot tell you anything yet but possibly in a year or so, your left eye may improve. Right now you have peripheral lower vision. I will release you from the hospital, but I want you to check with me for at least a year as we must wean you off the steroids.

Doctor, I am blind for all my life? I am blind! God help me!

CHAPTER I

How Did This Happen?

"Joe, walk me through those last days before you lost your sight. Help me understand why God would allow this to happen to you of all people."

I asked this question of Joe over and over during the last years of his life. Each time, his answer was exactly the same as though those days were indelibly stamped on his mind and in his heart. I believe the following account to be as near to Joe's answer as possible for me to remember.

How did all this happen? A very good question. I was taking communion to one of the shut-ins in Walterboro, South Carolina as part of my pastoral service at St. Anthony's Church. I can still recall how damp my clothes were and how difficult it was to breathe on that unusually hot and humid day. The following day, Thursday, I began to have a very severe sinus attack, or so I thought at the time. Everyone in the parish seemed to be suffering from the same allergy problems.

I called my doctor and received various medication and instructions to call back in a day or two if I had no relief. I don't recall returning the call, as I had to go out of town on a retreat for priests. It was the middle of August and from this time on, I began to have very severe headaches. Pounding, pounding, pounding like an oil derrick, never letting up.

The headaches continued each and every day. I could hardly sleep at night. Laying my head on the pillow seemed to aggravate the headache more than give it rest. I still told myself that this was sinus and would soon wear off. Still I thought it was odd that I had no nasal problems. The parish was very busy at this time, so I just put the thought out of my mind.

One morning, I had a very short period of double vision while I was shaving. I brought this to my doctor's attention, and an appointment with an ophthalmologist was set up for the next morning. I told the ophthalmologist about the headaches, the double vision, a constant pain in my jaw that made eating very painful, and my weight loss. I was given new eyeglasses but the pain persisted, and I was hardly able to do my job.

A few days later, Father Charles Day came by the Rectory in Walterboro and we went to lunch. Suddenly, during lunch, I could not see the golf course. This only lasted a few minutes. Returning to the Rectory, I felt that I had lost a little vision in both eyes. Fr. Day offered to cover for me over the weekend in the event that I would need help with the Masses. The next day, I called my physician and related the details of my incident the day before. I was sent to a second ophthalmologist. From there, I was sent to get a Computerized Tomography scan of the brain, see an Ear, Nose and Throat specialist, and also to see my dentist regarding jaw pain.

Later in the week, my vision became very fuzzy. I called the doctor and was told to see my regular ophthalmologist. As soon as my doctor looked into my eyes, he sent me immediately to Storm Eye Institute for consultation with their physicians. I was admitted to the hospital right away

I felt like an automobile being filled with high-test gasoline as the doctors tried to save as much of my vision as possible. My diagnosis was Temporal Arteritis. That evening, the Bishop came by for a visit. During this time, I began to lose my vision, but being a stubborn Irishman, I did not want to give in. I was now unable to see and was almost in total darkness. Strange to believe, but when I woke up in the morning, whether it was a dream or hallucination, I could see my room, the numbers on the telephone and the tiles on the floor.

In the meantime, there were a million different tests done by what seemed dozens of doctors. When I mentioned to them that in the early morning I was able to see my room, they could not understand it. But I know that for approximately thirty minutes after I would awaken, I could see my room, the clock in the hall, and the black and white tile floors. They would disappear as soon as the steroids were added to my IV The doctors then ordered a biopsy of an artery to be sure a correct diagnosis was made.

As the nurses prepared for the procedure, they became upset about my blood pressure. I tried to explain that since my heart attack in 1990, my pressure should not be taken on my left arm as this would be low and asked that they take it on my right arm. In the meantime, nurses and doctors were upset that my blood pressure had dropped so low. No one seemed to be listening to me and I began to wonder if I were actually speaking. Perhaps I was mute as well as being blind.

At this moment, my internist came in and reassured the staff. Happy to say, when they took pressure in my right arm everything and everyone was back to normal-blood pressure, nurses, and doctors. The biopsy showed that a correct diagnosis had been made and also a correct decision on steroid treatment. By now, vision in my right eye was totally gone, and there was very little vision in my left eye. Still, in my heart, I could not believe that I would never see again.

CHAPTER 2

The First Adjustment to Blindness

After Joe was put on a regular diet, someone would bring in the food tray and leave it at his bedside. The first days were rather rough, and it was difficult for him to find his food and eat being newly blind.

The first day he knocked his tray off the table. It made a terrible crash and all the nurses came running in, thinking he had fallen out of bed. They were very understanding and he was sent another meal.

One morning Joe could hardly wait for his pancake breakfast. He was feeling around the plate and poured what he thought was syrup on the pancakes. He called the nurse to ask what he had done wrong. They had a good laugh, as his grapefruit juice floated all over the plate and his tray.

At this time, one of the nurses explained how to view the plate as a clock-12, 3, 6, 9-and have some one identify where the food was in relation to the numbers.

Sometime later, perhaps two or three days, Joe was discharged from the hospital to the home of one of his very dear friends, he was in a terrible state of depression, but he was blessed to have friends to look after him.

While in the hospital, Joe was convinced that his sight would return in a few weeks at most. He had great faith that this was only a temporary medical setback.

CHAPTER 3

Depression

From the first day that Joe learned he was legally blind, he plunged into what he often referred to as his "Black Hell." During my visits to him in the hospital, he would grip my hand, almost breaking my fingers, and ask me over and over: *What will I do, where will I go, will I be able to survive? Take me God-Please just take me, don't leave me here blind and helpless!*

Before leaving his hospital room, I would always ask if there was something I could do for him.

Yes, he would always respond, *give me your eyes.*

I would try to tease him a little and answer, *You don't want my eyes. I can't see across the room. You want eyes with 20/20 vision!*

During the first year of his blindness, Joe had the additional misfortune of several fractured vertebrae following the large dose of steroids given to him immediately after his hospital admission. This setback caused both physical pain and mental anguish. He wondered if this were the way his life would be, one medical crisis after another until finally he would welcome death not as an enemy but as a friend.

Several times he said to me, *It is very difficult for me to take only one of my heart pills when I know I have a full bottle. Sometimes I feel like leaving this house and walking out back into the marsh and into the water over my head.*

Because I was always trying to get at least a small smile from him, I would answer, *Thank God the marsh is way in the back of your house, and you will never find it. You would walk around in circles for hours and someone would be sure to notice such bizarre behavior even from you!*

He would laugh and tell me I had no heart.

CHAPTER 4

Shame and Embarrassment

Father Joe was not by any means a proud man in the derogatory sense, but he was someone who took pride in both his appearance and his work.

He often admitted that having to be led like a child to and from the altar during Mass was very painful to him. The idea that hundreds of people were witnesses to his disability caused him great shame and embarrassment.

I would tell him he was an inspiration to these people and he should be proud of his ability to carry on with his ministry. His answer was always the same—*Easy for you to say.*

Joe hated that his loss of independence was made so public, but because he was a very strong man of great faith and a deep love for his God, he held his emotions deep in his heart and expressed only love and gratitude to those people who assisted him in his mission.

Perhaps his procession to and from the altar, always with assistance, was his personal walk with Christ—his personal "way of the cross."

CHAPTER 5

A Setback

In the mornings, Joe tried to get to the mailbox of the home where he was staying because he knew I would be on my "morning run" and pass him around 6 A.M. I would walk him around Indigo Point, about half a mile.

One morning after our walk, he had a very sharp pain in his back and thought he'd just twisted it the wrong way. However, the next day, while he took his shower, he had a tremendous pain in his back and had to lie down for a few minutes. To his surprise, he was unable to get off the bed without assistance. His doctor came by that evening and told him he would have to go to the hospital for X-rays. Much to his distress, he was informed that he had a fractured vertebra and would have to wear a back brace for a while.

This made him very, very depressed and he knew it was not easy on the family with whom he was staying.

I came by almost every day during my lunch hour to try and cheer him up with laughter and jokes. He likened my visits to medicine for the soul. Otherwise, he said, he would probably go to his room and cry several times a day.

One day, we had a long talk about miracles. Joe told me he always prayed for a miracle, all through the day and into the night until he fell asleep. I told him that I was glad that he prayed for a miracle that would return his vision, and that I prayed for the same miracle, too.

It was obvious that he was upset over the fact that he had begged God over and over for the return of his sight and God never seemed to respond. I asked him, *Joe, when you pray and you pray and you still cannot see, what do you do?*

I get very depressed, Joe answered. *I don't want to get out of bed in the morning; I just want to lie there and die!*

We walked for a few moments while I tried to think of something to say that might in some small way make an impression on him. Finally I said, *You know Joe, I want a miracle for you, too. Realistically, I believe the doctors are correct, and you are not going to be able to see any more than you do right now. I think that you should understand that if you plan to lie in bed until you die that it's not going to happen overnight. Who do you think is supposed to take care of you during this time? Are people supposed to just look the other way until they go in one day and find you dead? Joe, it hurts me to say this but no one owes it to you to have to wait on you hand and foot while you waste away. But you owe it to yourself, and you owe it to the fact that God has left you with the ability to get up in the morning, shower, dress, and go out to the kitchen for coffee.*

If you are going to have to live in this world, you must be a part of this world. You need to get with it. You must pick yourself up, brush off, and start again! I will quit my job to help you do this. I am sorry, but I will stop praying for the return of your sight, and instead I will pray for the return of your life. I hope you understand that this is tough love. You have been blind for a year now, and we have to stop praying and start working, as I believe that this is God's plan for you.

Forgive me, Joe, for being so frank, and forgive me, God, if I have misunderstood the signs.

Joe often said in the following months that he thought about that conversation a great deal. No one was obligated to take care of him and he knew he had to begin taking care of himself.

There were times when I felt that I was a little hard on Joe, but it was clear to me that he would never get over this terrible depression on his own and maybe, because of the long years of being friends, God thought that I was one of the few people that he would listen too.

Joe often said to me, *No one in the world except you, Betty, would have the courage to speak like that to a blind person, particularly to a poor blind priest!!*

The one thing in life I have never been able to hold is my tongue and in the almost 40 years that Joe and I were friends, we had many wonderful discussions, debates, and arguments where we both felt we were right. This was one time when I felt that I won...if not the war, at least this battle.

As the summer came, Joe realized he would have to leave the house in which he was staying and make other arrangements. He took a trip to Chicago to visit family and await his fate. He received a call from the diocese informing him that if he wished to return to Charleston, the Pastor, had invited Joe to live in the Rectory of the Church of the Nativity. Joe was delighted with this news, as he had spent several years as pastor of this parish and knew the people.

CHAPTER 6

Melonie Pinckney

I love Melonie as if she were my own daughter.

Joe said this time and again during the years that Melonie was employed as the housekeeper at the Church of the Nativity. He looked forward to her arrival every morning so that they could have their coffee and cigarette break before the day began. She took care of his needs as far as food and laundry, and she also read from the Missal, the texts that Joe would need in order to give a small sermon during his daily and Sunday Masses.

It is difficult to describe other peoples' feelings for one another. God must have had a hand in putting Melonie in that house at that particular time. She and I had many conversations about what to do or not to do for Joe. She was one of the most conscientious and devoted people in Joe's world and he thanked her from the bottom of his heart. Melonie told me a little about her relationship with Fr. Maher.

"When I heard that Fr. Maher was coming to live at Nativity Rectory, I was very nervous. I didn't know him and had no idea what to expect. Would I know the correct things to say and do for him?

I did a little research and learned what I could about blindness. The day Fr. Maher arrived, I think he was a little nervous about me as well. But that nervousness went away for both of us on the following day as we sat and talked about organizing his closet so that he could easily match up his clothes. We hit it off very quickly—kindred souls, I suppose.

Fr. Maher was strong, loving, understanding, funny, and very smart. I admired him for how devoted he was to the people of all the parishes where he had served. Without smothering him, I tried to do little things that the seeing often do not think about. For example, I adjusted the dial on the heating and air conditioning system so that Fr. Maher knew that turning the dial right (or toward hell, as we referred to it) turned the heat up.

I think Fr. Maher helped me much more than I helped him. While he was adjusting to his blindness, he also guided me through a very emotional time in my life. During our morning chats, we both would let go of a few of our anxieties and refill ourselves with love.

The time we shared was so special to me because I know Fr. Maher loved and respected me as a person. He validated my worth. All of my memories of Fr. Maher are special because I loved and admired him so very much."

Melonie Pinckney now runs a business with her husband and has returned to college because her friend, Fr. Maher, inspired her to be the best she can be.

CHAPTER 7

Describing Himself as Blind

When Joe referred to himself as being blind, his agony was evident in the tone of his voice. His voice broke every time he used the word blind. I can close my eyes and remember the look that came over his face. Pain, frustration, and hopelessness. The pain and frustration he could deal with. If only he had hope.

At one point he spoke about having to live without hope and compared hopelessness with being one of the "living dead."

"I never feared facing the end of my life," he said, *"but I expected it to end in the grave, not in this black Hell that I exist in. I gave my life to God and to the church, and I asked for very little for myself in return. Now I find myself blind, and I cry out day and night, but God does not seem to be in my life at all. I feel deep anger toward God and, at times, I deny his existence. But in the end, I'm on my knees again begging for His help and His strength to go on. Oh God, what a life. What a hell of a life."*

CHAPTER 8

The Working Priest

Joe thought his blindness meant the end of his priestly duties, but God had other plans. Thanks to the assistance of his friends, Sister Noreen, Phillip Noe, and Dan Sullivan, Joe was able to return to the altar, saying Mass on Sundays as well as during the week. Joe always referred to Phil as his right-hand man. The people at Church of the Nativity loved Joe's three-minute sermons, and visitors were amazed to find he was blind.

Thanks to his faithful drivers, he was able to visit the shut-ins of the parish. Because Joe himself was a prisoner in his room, he was unable to go out on his own. Through his own trials, he was able to empathize with his parishioners and they with him.

He loved the times he spent in Nativity's school. The children had a wonderful relationship with "Father Joe," and they were not at all uncomfortable with his blindness. The lower grades were his favorites, and these children asked many questions about how he managed to get around and go places. Some of their questions included: "Father, how do you go to the bathroom? How do you know it's time to go to bed if you can't tell it's nighttime?"

I taught Joe how to do the Macarena, and he delighted the younger children by dancing with them in the classroom. He enjoyed the older kids, too, but their sessions were more serious and more concerned with the problems of growing up in today's world.

Joe was also delighted when different pastors would invite him to assist them at their Reconciliation Services.

The guys will hold the service, he would tell me excitedly, *and then we will go out to dinner or maybe we will eat before the service.* I often wondered if the priests realized how desperately Joe wanted to return to being just "one of the guys."

With Sister Noreen and Philip Noe at his side, Joe was able to serve the people of Nativity parish until his death.

CHAPTER 9

Angels of the Night

On three different occasions, Joe either fell or almost fell while trying to make his way back to the rectory from the church after dark. He and I had many squabbles regarding his walking alone in the dark, but he was determined not to inconvenience anyone by asking them to walk him home.

The first two times, he was rescued by neighbors who happened to be driving by and saw him fall. They were very kind, explaining that they were not members of his church but knew who he was and that he was blind.

The third time he became disoriented after stepping off the walk. He stepped into the grass, walking deep into the wooded area heading toward a very large ditch at the end of the property.

Suddenly, he heard a *chorus of angels shouting, "Father! Stop! Don't move!"* It was a parishioner and her children, friends of Joe. I finally convinced him that he should take people up on their offers to walk him home. Joe was very grateful to these people whom he called his angels of the night.

CHAPTER 10

Sins of Omission

Do Catholics still believe in "sins of omission?" I recall being taught that there are such sins and, as a child, I was much more impressed with these sins rather than the sins spoken of as mortal. It's much easier to understand neglecting, disregarding, and ignoring others than it is to imagine murder and adultery.

There were many times when I dropped the ball with Joe. Not doing things or going places I knew he'd enjoy, because sometimes I just didn't want to be bothered. Though it's too late to correct this with a man who was always content to do what ever I wanted, I can only hope that my failures will prove to be a learning experience.

One incident in particular still haunts me, and even though I apologized for days, I still have regrets. Joe called me to let me know that he would not be able to visit a shut-in because his driver was unavailable that afternoon. He was disappointed, but he was more concerned that his driver might be ill as no excuse had been given for his absence.

The next day when I picked up Joe, he asked me to read the obituary page from the newspaper to him. This was the only way he had of keeping up "with who was alive and who was dead." At the time, I was busy and put off reading to him. The next day I took a quick look, called Joe, and said no one had died from Nativity. He was satisfied and didn't ask any questions about any other deaths in other parishes, and I didn't offer any information.

The next week, Joe's driver returned and said he was sorry to have let Joe down the week before, but his brother from another parish had died. Joe was not only hurt, but also terribly embarrassed that this driver had been so good and faithful for months, and he had not even attended the brother's wake or funeral. I felt it was my fault. One of the few things Joe ever asked of me was to be told when someone he knew passed away to take him to the services.

This sort of thing happened to Joe several times and was just another cause of his spending many hours of extreme mental suffering, trying to find answers to his one big question, "Why me, Lord, why me?"

CHAPTER 11

Do I Look Odd To Others?

My husband, Frank, and I always told Joe that he did not appear to look "odd" or handicapped. We reminded him how shocked people were to learn of his blindness after seeing him say Mass or even on the dance floor. We felt that it was important for Joe not to feel self-conscious, awkward, or even ashamed of his blindness when we took him out. He hated the white cane, and we never made him use it. Because we loved him, we understood and respected his feelings.

We did take the cane on all air flights in a carry-on bag. He'd lean on it at the gate, and we would be ushered in before other passengers. Joe always got a great laugh at this.

One day while walking in Holy Cross Cemetery on James Island in Charleston, I let go of Joe's hand and told him that from this time on, when we walked on a wide street or road that he must walk alone with only slight assistance from me. *Hold your head up, chest out, swing your arms, breathe deep, and be a free spirit.*

He loved this and I tried not to even touch him unless a car was coming. One day while walking free and enjoying himself, Joe mentioned how much he missed driving his car.

Joe, you can drive my car here in the cemetery" I replied. *You remember the road, and I'll just caution you to turn left to 10 o'clock. Go toward 12 o'clock!*

Joe really laughed at the thought and said, *Well, even if I run over someone, they can't say I killed them!*

So on two different occasions, an automobile was going around Holy Cross, driven by a blind man. On one of our drives a gentleman whom I knew from my days working at St. Francis Hospital in downtown Charleston (a Catholic Hospital run by the Sisters of Charity of our Lady of Mercy) rode by on his bicycle and as a joke told me to get my car off the roadway. Joe laughed and shouted back, *If you knew what we knew, you would get yourself off this road!*

Later as we talked about the drive, I could tell by the tears in Joe's eyes that this was a very emotional experience. He never asked to drive again, and I think he must have considered my actions an answer to one of his special prayers: *Lord, if only I could drive again, just one more time before I die.*

CHAPTER 12

How We Filled the Days

Special events, such as out-of-town or out-of-state travels were easy-plan, pack, and go. Day to day amusement was a little more difficult. Though Joe was delighted just to get out of the house, I always felt that each day should be special but very low key.

Sometimes we would drive up to Jeanie Urtz's house in Georgetown. Several friends would come over, we would sit around and talk, go out to lunch, and leave for Charleston in the late afternoon loaded down with Jean's homemade cookies. What a treat!

Other times, we drove down to Beaufort. We would sit in a swing at the waterfront park, and I would describe the boats at the marina, people fishing, and people just sitting or walking in the park. Then we'd walk along the main street and shop a bit before going into Joe's favorite restaurant. We'd drive back home along Highway 17 and, since he was very familiar with this area, I would tell about which buildings were still there, which were gone, and what was built since he had lost his sight. I soon realized he was uncomfortable with the "new" things along the road. He seemed more content remembering things as he saw them in the past.

We spent a lot of time walking in James Island Park. Joe really loved to go there and for a while, he was able to walk three miles around the trail without stopping to rest. This was not to be in the last year of his life, as he seemed to lose stamina very rapidly during those last 9-10 months.

Joe loved it when we would pass a shelter where people were eating and listening to music. I'd make him stop walking, and we would dance to whatever kind of music happened to be playing. Sometimes fast, sometimes slow.

Several times, we were discovered by people we knew as we danced along the hiking trails. Many times, we were seen by children from Nativity school. They really loved catching Father Maher dancing in the park.

We also spent many days walking on Folly Beach, since Joe loved the ocean and would try his best to see a little out of his one eye that still had some small vision.

We also would go downtown, sometimes parking on the Battery and sometimes parking in Cathedral churchyard. We'd always walk to a local shop so I could buy my Irish import coffee beans. Then we'd have lunch, usually on the porch of one of Joe's favorite restaurants.

It was very difficult to walk Joe in the city, any city, but we never gave up. First, we had to deal with the usual sidewalk clutter, signs, benches, and planters. Then we have to avoid trees with low hanging branches, flowers, etc. We also had to contend with pedestrian traffic (difficult on narrow sidewalks). There were street crossings, steps up, and steps downs, look both ways, uneven sidewalks, and more. I always spent a lot of time pulling, pushing, and sometimes swearing under my breath, but Joe always apologized for not being able to see and not being able to take care of himself. In the end, we'd laugh and joke that once again we had conquered King Street.

It is only now that I realize that for four years no matter where in the world we were, I only saw gray sidewalks and blacktop roads. Strange I didn't notice that before now.

CHAPTER 13

Helping Me Around the House

Joe loved helping me around the house, not because he liked to work, but because this was something he could get lots of mileage from. It began by his offering to help me because I did not want to hire professional help. I think his idea was to wash a few dishes after meals. He did wash dishes, but he also washed windows, woodwork, and my car. He cut my lawn with me following behind, yelling, "Go left...go right." He also helped prepare meals by cutting vegetables for salads and setting the table. He particularly liked to help with the Christmas baking. He always went home with a full stomach and a bag of goodies.

He loved this labor (as he referred to it), as it gave him great subjects for his sermons on Sunday. He could complain to a captive audience.

CHAPTER 14

Ireland 1996

On Christmas Day 1995, Frank and I told Joe that we were planning a trip to Ireland in the late summer, and we wanted him to go with us. I believe he went home that night and began to pack.

The day after Christmas, he called me around 7:45 P.M.

Where are you people? He asked. *I've been packed and ready to go since 5 A.M.!!*

He talked about nothing else for months and could hardly wait for early September, the time we had decided on for our holiday. He planned what he would do, relatives he would visit, and friends of ours he would finally get to meet. We stayed busy all summer making reservations for our flight, getting Joe a passport, and buying him some new clothes.

Frank was great when we took Joe shopping for clothes. He helped Joe into the changing room, set out the new clothes, and then waited while Joe changed. Then he brought Joe out into the sales area so we could look over the pants to be sure they fit. Joe thanked Frank over and over again, saying, "I am such a bother."

Frank would answer, *that's OK Joe, you can buy lunch today. That's the trade off"* We got a good laugh all summer as Joe counted down the days until we flew to Shannon, Ireland.

Joe and Frank talked about working as a team to prevent my spending all of the money shopping one he first day we arrived in Ireland. *Joe, we don't stand a chance,* Frank would say. *She'll spend all of her money, then all of mine, and finally all of yours!*

Hell no! Joe always responded. *She may spend her money and she may spend yours, but I'll be damned if she'll spend mine!*

Finally, the day arrived and we left Charleston for Shannon, Ireland. Joe was so excited. It was all he could do to stay in his seat on the plane.

When we arrived in Shannon, a very dear friend, Father John Dunne, an Irish priest from County Cork who served in the Missions in Africa, met us at the airport. John traveled with us for the first four days and made a delightful guide and driver. He had the most wonderful sense of humor and kept us entertained the entire time.

Joe thought John was fantastic, and he was very interested in his work in Africa. John, on the other hand, was astonished at how well Joe could cope and how willing he was to "go with the flow."

During the entire trip, we stayed in a different home or Bed and Breakfast almost every night. John and Frank were amazed at how after two or three minutes of instructions, Joe was able to stand at the side of his bed, walk to the wall, and turn left or right as needed to go to the bathroom. In the bathroom, I would show him where the shower, sink, and toilet was, lay out his shaving kit and clothes for the next day. Joe would be so pleased in the morning when one of us would look in on him with a cup of coffee. He would be sitting, waiting, having showered, shaved, packed, and dressed.

After John left us, we began working our way east to Dublin and our friends. We stopped overnight in Monaghan with the O'Connor family, where we had a grand visit, going to a beautiful park and taking a wonderful tour around Castle Leslie. Joe enjoyed his visit very much and promised to return another time.

As we traveled across Ireland, surely one of the most

beautiful countries in the world, we were lucky because Joe, while attending seminary in England, had made several visits to Ireland. He remembered the beauty of the countryside. One day, we helped him climb up a very rocky hillside that looked out over the Atlantic Ocean. I described the land, the rough sea crashing on the rocks, birds flying over, and a few seals in the water.

I see it in my mind, Joe said as he squeezed my hand. *I see it in my mind.*

There were tears in all of our eyes as we climbed down that hill, and I heard Joe whisper, *Why me, God, why me?*

In Dublin, my friends, Jackie Shannon and the O'Sullivan family greeted us. We had a wonderful week traveling around, taking pictures, and visiting friends in their homes. Everyone was astonished at how Joe adapted to the changes in his living quarters. Joe loved everything about Dublin and our friends, especially Jackie, whom he called his Irish Colleen.

We left Dublin and went South to visit Sister Noreen, who was in Youghal, Cork, visiting her mother. Sister Noreen's mother was very ill, and Joe was delighted that he was able to visit her and give her a special blessing. Father John Dunne joined us again and also said a special prayer for Sr. Noreen's mother. Then we were off to County Tipperary to the town of Killenaule, the birthplace of Joe's parents.

Joe's visit to Killenaule was one of the highlights of our trip. Though he had visited the town on two different occasions while studying in England, he was still very interested in hearing descriptions of the town and surrounding countryside. Most of Joe's relatives had passed away, but we spent a delightful afternoon with his cousin in her home.

We went into the town to visit the church where Joe's parents were baptized. Joe climbed into the pulpit with the aid of Father John Dunne and had a grand time preaching "fire and brimstone" to an imaginary congregation. We were able to locate the graves of his grandparents and several aunts and uncles, and we visited the parish school that his parents attended. Fortunately, the church and school were on the street, but the graveyard was all uphill behind the church. We had quite a time between Father John, Frank, and me keeping Joe on his feet.

We also had the opportunity to visit the house where Joe's father was born. It was very touching to see him run his hand across the old wooden door and across the windowsill. Later on, he told us that, at that moment, he felt very close to his dad, almost as if he were there with us.

After our visit to Killenaule, we had to part company with Father John. We were all sad to see him go, but as Joe said, he helped to make our trip the wonderful adventure it was. So we went on to Bunratty Castle Banquet, and our last night in Ireland.

The Castle Banquet was wonderful! We were greeted by bagpipers and led into the castle and up a flight of wooden stairs to the receiving area. Here we were introduced to the castle singers and musicians who served us cups of mead, a wine that dates back to medieval times. After all the guests had arrived for the banquet, we were invited to the Banquet Hall at the top of the castle.

One of the entertainers came over and told Joe he could ride up a small elevator. We wanted Joe to enjoy the full experience, so we declined the offer. Boy, were we wrong!

First of all, the stairs were in the tower of the castle, and I doubt that the distance from side to side was three feet, so I could not walk beside Joe. Then the steps were stone and at least 10-12 inches high going round and round in semi-darkness. This meant that the person in front and above you could possibly kick you in the chest and you could do the same to the person behind. So there we were, having enjoyed the mead and now having to climb these stairs—stairs that were only about half the width of your shoe so you never felt really secure as you stepped higher and higher.

Every so often as we climbed, we came to a high opening that led to nowhere (maybe used as an exit if the castle was under attack). About a dozen times as Joe saw the outside light in front of him, he tried to step out and fall from the side of the castle. We had all of these people in the stairway yelling, pulling, and dragging him back into the building. Everyone was laughing and carrying on as Joe kept shouting, *Let me go. I'm heading to the light, my time has come.*

In spite of everything, Joe was a great sport and the people around us thought it really funny that this blind priest was "heading for the light." Needless to say, Joe was a very popular fellow at the banquet. He told several people that he wasn't really blind but was a part of the entertainment. They never found out differently. This delighted Joe.

Father Joe and Father John Dunne

Sister Noreen Buttimer, Father Joe and friends

CHAPTER 15

Two Weddings-Family of the Heart Gary White and Holly M. Davis Barbara White and Charles Thompson

Barbara White and Gary White are our grandchildren. These two weddings are the only two weddings that Joe performed after the loss of his sight. He did this only because of his affection for all our children for they were like family to him.

Holly Davis and Gary White were married in Blessed Sacrament Church in Charleston, South Carolina in November 1996. Joe assisted Pastor Father Francis Hanley. This was Joe's first wedding ceremony since losing his sight.

Gary drove Joe crazy during those last weeks, as he had to keep rescheduling the Pre-Cana meeting that all Catholics are obligated to attend prior to marriage in the church.

Gary, I swear to God, if I were the priest in charge of this wedding, I'd toss you out the back door! Joe exclaimed. I'm sure Father Hanley felt the same, but Gary and Holly attended the session at the very last minute.

Joe married Barbara White and Charlie Thompson in a garden ceremony at their home in Ravenel, South Carolina. Joe did a wonderful job of obtaining permission from the Bishop as well as from the pastor of the parish where the wedding would take place. We went down to the Chancery Office and picked up all the necessary paperwork. Joe sat down with Barbara and

Charlie and explained the church's position on mixed marriages, took care of all the paper work, helped them choose readings, and assisted in planning a most beautiful and touching wedding. Dozens of people came to Joe after the service to congratulate him and to say how amazed they were to hear that he was blind. Much credit must go to Frank's sister-in-law, Sandra, who prompted Joe during the ceremony.

Holly, Gary, Barbara, and Charlie will never forget how much Joe loved them and how proud he was of them.

One day after Gary teased him about not having the White DNA, Joe replied, *DNA only counts if they are trying to catch you in a paternity case. Family is family of the heart, and that's what we are.*

Holly, Gary and Father Joe
dancing the Macarena

Father Joe, Father Hanley, Holly and Gary

Father Joe, Barbara and Charlie

CHAPTER 16
Holidays

Joe spent all holidays with my family. On July 4 and Labor Day, we always went to the Elks' or the Knights of Columbus' picnics. Other holidays were spent in our home with all the family coming together. On Thanksgiving in 1996, we had all our family, including Frank's brother and sister-in-law, Nelson and Sandy, plus about 25 young people from Florida for Gary and Holly's wedding. Joe was in his glory as all the young people laughed and joked with him, teased him unmercifully, and made sure he was part of their conversations.

Before Christmas or Joe's birthday, my family always asked, "What does Joe need?" His answer was always the same. *A new pair of eyes.* He usually celebrated Christmas with a special Mass in our dining room, and that made the holiday even more special.

Joe and I had a great time doing his Christmas shopping. For years, we bought gifts for different people, and always golf balls for Frank. But in 1997, Joe began to fade a little and was not up to shopping trips that lasted two or three days. Instead we went to the Hickory Farms shop at the mall and bought 22 baskets of cheese and meat. They made great gifts.

One by one, Joe gave his baskets to drivers, friends, and parishioners.

Come over to the Rectory, he's say. *I have a gift for you.* Then he'd call me and let me know whose name to mark off his Christmas list.

Joe was one of the most generous people I've ever known. If Frank or I ever expressed a desire for anything, Joe would argue that he should be allowed to buy it for us. *God knows you deserve it for all that you two do for me,* Joe would exclaim.

The first Christmas after Joe died was very difficult, but we felt that he kept his promise to always be with us in spirit. "Love is stronger than death" (Song of Songs 8:6).

CHAPTER 17

Frank and Joe

Frank and Joe had a special kind of friendship. They talked sports, mainly golf, and the usual subjects that guys like to discuss. Frank is a wonderful loving man, and this gentle side of his personality acted as Joe's caregiver.

On Sunday afternoons, they would watch golf on TV. Frank would explain every play-who was teeing off, how far the ball would go, whether it landed on the green or in the rough. Joe was able to follow the game, laughing and cheering for his favorite players.

On several occasions, I watched the two of them play golf in our backyard. Frank would put the golf ball on the ground at Joe's feet, then he would line Joe up, touch the ball with the head of the club, and help Joe bring the club up to his shoulder for the shot. Joe usually hit the ball so there would be lots of cheering and applause.

Occasionally I suggested that I ask a friend to have Joe over so that Frank and I could have some time alone or go away for a weekend. Frank always said, *No, I hate to see a grown man cry. We can't just go off without him. He's no trouble, and it would break his heart if we left him behind.*

Because of Frank's wonderful gift of caring, we took Joe everywhere-Ireland, Washington, D.C., and St. Simons Island. Every summer, we drove to Chicago so Joe could visit his family.

I have many memories of Frank assisting Joe, but none are as touching as those times when Joe would ask to be assisted to the men's room. Regardless of where we were, a crowded restaurant, an Irish pub on St. Patrick's day, a castle banquet in Ireland, a concert at James Island County Park, a dance at the Elks Lodge, Frank would put his elbow out for Joe to hold onto and he would walk Joe to and from the restroom.

One Sunday our parish had a reception for our pastor's birthday. I was busy serving food along with members of our Women's Guild. Frank was to pick up Joe so the two of them could go home and wait for me. Just after the reception began, I saw Frank in the church kitchen trying to signal me to come over. He said that when he went to pick Joe up at the Rectory, he was shocked to see Joe's hair, face, shirt, and hands covered in blood.

Joe explained that he had walked into the door between his bedroom and bath. He didn't realize how much his head had bled, so he only wiped his forehead with his face cloth. Frank took him back into the house, washed his face and hair and found a clean shirt. He also washed out Joe's bloody shirt. Frank was very anxious that I check Joe's head to determine whether or not he needed stitches. The wound was not that deep, but Frank was prepared to spend the day in the emergency room with Joe if needed.

What can you say about a man like this? Joe often said that Frank has all the qualities of a saint and the most endearing is his humility. Joe was humble himself, and he admired people who spent their lives trying to do the right thing, never asking anything in return.

CHAPTER 18

Body Language

We may think that only sighted people are able to communicate thoughts by way of body language. This is not true, as Joe and I developed a great way of communication. Not with words, but by touch.

When I walked with Joe, I held his hand and tucked his arm under mine, bending at the elbow. This made it easy for me to move him about. Initially I would say, *Move right Joe* or *Move left, step up, step down, stop.* This always meant that conversation must stop while instructions are given.

Almost without realizing it, I began to pull Joe into me to avoid incoming pedestrian traffic, plants, or anything he might run into. It was very funny because when I would pull him against me, he would pull back and shout, *Oh Boy!!*

I would slap his hand and call him "a dirty old man" and then explain to him that this was a signal for him to move over. Slowly, without my being aware of it, Joe began to respond to a slight tug toward or away from me and move right or left as indicated. A slight pull back with my arm, and he would slow his pace and prepare to stop. A slight pressure down with my hand and he would step down, slight pressure up and he would step up. In this way, we were able to go downtown, maneuver around all sorts of obstacles, cross streets, and go up and down stairs without having to make Joe even more aware of his limitations.

I remember being amazed when I realized how well he could

interpret my moves without either one of us being aware of it. I believe that this came about because we spent hours and hours walking together. I also believe that Joe had great confidence in me to be able to relax and follow me without question. Frank and Joe were also beginning to be able to communicate in this way, but Frank insists that I make it clear that Joe only held his elbow. They did not hold hands!

In an attempt to help Joe maintaining his dignity and a feeling of independence, I agreed to accept a stipend for taking care of him two of the five days that he spent with us every week. Because Frank played golf three days a week and cooked at the Elks Lodge every other Thursday for their dinner meeting, Joe and I spent more time together. There is no way you can be sure a blind person is doing well unless you are constantly in touch. Frank and I were with Joe every weekend, every holiday, any time the housekeeper was out sick or on vacation, all day every Tuesday and Thursday, and every Friday night. On Monday and Wednesday I called Joe at least a half dozen times during the day and evening. We agreed this was the only way we could be sure he was OK. Frank and I considered this level of care giving a privilege not a burden.

When I think of all the things I miss about Joe, one of the most painful is the loss to my sense of touch. After spending years holding hands and touching instead of always speaking, losing Joe meant I had to grieve the loss of that sense of touch.

CHAPTER 20
What If?

Before and after going blind, Joe lived with courage, dignity, and humor. But sometimes he felt haunted by fears-the indignity of being helpless and the fear that he no longer had any real worth in the world.

He worried about what he would do if he had to move from the Nativity Rectory. He worried that the current pastor would be transferred to another parish and that a new pastor might not be as hospitable. These fears grew as each new transfer of pastors was announced.

I could never help Joe understand what an asset he was at Nativity Church. We always assured him that we would always have a place for him and we would cross that bridge when we came to it. He still continued to wonder where God was during those last years of frustration, anger, depression, despair, and fear of the future. Fear of what would happen to him before he finally died.

CHAPTER 21

I'm Still the Same Person

Joe only wanted to be treated as normal. He knew that some people would shy away in sympathy. Nevertheless, he wanted people to stop and chat, drop in for a visit, or make a phone call. He often said, *I'm still the same as always. Why can't they see and understand? Just because I'm blind doesn't mean I'm dead.*

Not long after Joe settled into his life at Nativity Church, I had occasion to call the diocese on Joe's behalf. I was reading our diocese newspaper and discovered a very nice article about a gentleman from one of the parishes in the upper part of the state. The thing that caught my eye was a little box on the bottom of the page asking readers to send in the name of anyone whose story might be of interest as it related to the work of the church.

I shot to the telephone and God bless the young lady who answered. She really caught it from me. I told her I could not believe that the paper was actually soliciting stories when right in her own city was a blind priest who was saying Mass, hearing confession, visiting and ministering to shut-ins, and teaching in the school one or two days a week. The young lady was very kind and promised to get my request in right away.

The second time I contacted the diocese came after Joe found out, quite by accident, that one of his fellow priests had been ill in the hospital. I asked him if it was the policy that newsletters went out to priests notifying them of this sort of thing, and he informed me that he had been dropped from the mailing list following his diagnosis.

To the phone again!! I had no idea who to call, so I spoke to a friend who worked at the chancery. She promised to check when she went into work the next day and get back to me. When she called the next day, she assured me that she put Joe back on the mailing list. I asked that she have whoever took him off the mailing list to call me.

I wanted to tell that person that dead people are blind, but blind people are not dead. Blind people still care what goes on in the world. They still care what goes on in the lives of the people whom they care about. Joe often said I was the only guardian angel who came equipped with a sword.

CHAPTER 22

Joe's Health

In the fall of 1997, Joe began to show slight signs of change in energy and endurance. This decline was gradual and perhaps not noticed by anyone other than Frank and me.

In January of 1998, Joe had a rather unexpected incident in our house, which was very upsetting to all of us.

One evening, out of the blue, Joe asked me, *Why did I have to assist with the Baptism at the church today?* I looked at Frank and I could see the surprised look on his face. *Joe,* I replied, *don't you remember that the pastor is away for a few days?* Joe was shocked. *Away!* He almost shouted the word. *What do you mean away?*

I asked Joe several questions pertaining to things that happened during the past three or four months and he had absolutely no recall. He didn't even remember that we drove him to Chicago four months before.

I called Joe's doctor, went back to Joe, made him stand and walk, grip my hands, and all of these actions were normal. But still he had no short-term memory of the past few months.

The doctor told me to keep Joe at my house for several days, observe him carefully, and if there were no problems during the night, have him at the hospital the next day for tests. Joe's episode lasted exactly 30 minutes.

We went to the hospital early the next morning where we stayed for about five hours. Joe first had a CAT Scan of the brain followed by an MRI. Joe was a wonderful man in every area except patience. Every five minutes he'd say, *Lets get the hell out of this place. I'm not waiting all day for these people to move.*

Finally I said, *OK Joe, we are leaving now. We are in the parking lot headed for my car.* This would infuriate him but also make him laugh. After we went through this same routine five or six times, he finally settled down to just sitting and waiting.

His physician called me later that afternoon and told me what I already suspected. Joe had suffered a small stroke but was now past any danger and would probably be fine. *What do you want to do?* the doctor asked.

I don't want to do anything at all, I replied. That's the way we left it. We told no one. But I told Joe if anyone in authority called me and said they heard a rumor he'd been at the hospital all day, or that they had received a statement from Joe's insurance, I would tell the truth at that time. I insisted that Joe call his brother and tell him of his temporary loss of memory and subsequent hospital tests. In the end, no one asked, so the event was never mentioned outside of our home.

Joe gradually lost strength as the months went by. I had already told him we'd go to Ireland in June to visit our new great granddaughter, but I had many fears about taking Joe on such a long, exhausting trip. The only thing Frank had to say about it was that if we left Joe behind, it would kill him and I believed this was true.

I thought about it and prayed about it. Finally, I said, *Lord, if Joe drops dead in Ireland, he'll be doing the things he loves with the people he loves and that is all that really matters.*

CHAPTER 23

Ireland 1998

When our great granddaughter, Regan White, was born in April 1998, we knew we had to return to Dublin to visit our grandson Gary, and his wife, Holly. Joe was delighted when we asked him to go along with us. By now, he was beginning to feel very much at home in Ireland. We have many friends there, and he knew that our friends were also his friends.

We arrived in Dublin in June 1998. Granddaughter Barbara and husband Charlie were already there so we had a few days together in the Olde Sod before Charlie and Barbara had to return to Charleston. We were together with old friends Jackie Shannon, Peggy O'Sullivan, and all of the O'Sullivan family, so Joe was constantly surrounded by the people he loved. This was Joe's greatest desire, to always be able to reach out and touch another person since he hated being alone.

And so it was that we went out every day to parks, castles, downtown, trips to see friends in other cities, and always our friends and family loving Joe and being loved in return. He was delighted with Regan. He rocked her to sleep, held her hand while we rode in the car, and to his great joy, he, Frank, and I went along with Holly and Regan to the American Embassy the day Regan received her American Citizenship papers making her a citizen of both the United States and Ireland.

We returned to our favorite Bed and Breakfast in Blackrock. On one of our trips around the country, Frank, Joe, and I went to Ballybunion Golf course in County Kerry. Joe kept asking if we had enough time for a round or two. What a sight that would have been, a blind man playing the Old Ballybunion Course.

Joe decided he wanted to eat nothing but peanut butter and jam sandwiches whenever we went out to eat. Regardless of where we were, from the grand hotels to the pubs, we would have to open the car trunk and I would stand on the street making the sandwiches that he would brazenly take into restaurants and shamelessly ask for a plate and a drink. If anyone questioned this, and some defiantly did, he told them he was on a special diet.

We had many great adventures with Joe on this trip, but the heartache was that he was obviously not well and he was making a great effort to keep up with everyone. We would have to stop every 10-15 minutes for him to sit down and rest. Joe had a wonderful visit, but he said several times on the flight home that he knew he'd never return to Ireland and see his friends again. I thought he was just depressed to be leaving it all behind, but maybe he knew something I didn't.

The Ireland trip was tiring for Joe, but as we got on the plane in Dublin to return home, he said to me, *'It was all I prayed it would be and more. I know you people had to take it easy because of me, and I thank you from the bottom of my heart.*

After we returned home in July, Joe never really returned to his normal routine. It was extremely hot in Charleston, and the heat seemed to drain all of his energy. Still he never once complained. Joe was just happy to continue to be able to do the things he had to do, explaining, *I'm getting slow but then I'm getting old too.*

During this time, Frank and I saw something coming, we just didn't know what. Because Joe had one ambulatory surgery and was facing another, there were plenty of physicians visits, lab work, EKGs, and chest X-rays. Everything came back normal.

We never left Joe alone in the Rectory at night if the pastor was out of town and not expected to return in the evening. We would pick Joe up very later at night and return him very early the next morning. No one ever knew that he was away and this was the way he wanted it. He would laugh and say, *The neighbors see some woman sneaking me out at 10:30 P.M. and back in at 6:30 A.M. I hope they think I'm having an affair.*

I was afraid for Joe to be alone at night. Not so much because he might become ill, but that there might be a fire in the house. There was no way that Joe could have gotten out of that house alive in the event of a fire. The only reason Joe would agree to come to our house overnight was because he too was terrified of the idea of a fire.

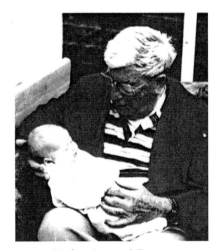

Father Joe and Regan

CHAPTER 24

Planning for Surgery

Joe's CAT Scan and MRI from January 1998 showed a Mass in his parotid artery that would require surgery. I took Joe to the hospital and a biopsy was taken which showed no cancer at the time. This was good news since Joe did not want to have surgery during the Lenten season. We went to several different physicians during this period and all reports were normal.

There was no pressure to have surgery within the next few months as long as Joe was followed by his physicians. Finally the surgery was scheduled for September 8th, a Tuesday, the day after Labor Day. Once again, we had all sorts of lab work, X-rays, and cardiograms. All results were normal.

Joe spent several days with us before surgery and on Labor Day we went to the Elks Picnic. Joe looked great that day and everyone remarked on how handsome he was in his straw hat and sunglasses. That night, he went to bed early in anticipation of being at the ambulatory unit of the hospital by 6:00 A.M.

We got up early and Joe was signed into the hospital without incident. I stayed with him until they took him into the surgical area, and then waited along with Joe's friends, Frances Frizelle, Mary Soffera, and Pauline Bissey.

Joe's doctor stopped by to check on Joe and said he was fine and surgery would be over shortly. Not long after that, the surgeon came out, told us that Joe did great, did not have any cancer, and sent us back to visit him and assure him all was well.

The others went home, and I stayed with Joe who had been admitted to the hospital for an overnight stay.

The next morning, Joe was discharged home to my house and per his doctor, he was to stay at least a week. The surgery took four hours so he would have a moderate amount of pain and taking medication would make it unsafe for him to be alone.

Joe did very well for the next few days considering the surgery. He was weak and the medication made him drowsy. The large incision and drainage tube from the neck did nothing to enhance his looks. He had several visitors during this time and also enjoyed a visit from his friend, Phil Noe. All of this activity made the days go by quickly.

On Friday morning, Joe and I had an argument about when he should return to the rectory. He was adamant he should go home so he could hear confession on Saturday and say Mass on Sunday. I tried to point out to him that he was in no condition to go back to work, but he became so upset I agreed to taking him home Friday afternoon and return on Saturday morning to see how he was and then decide what to do.

I was in contact with him by telephone two or three times during that Friday evening and at 10 P.M., he called to say he was going to bed and would call me as soon as he awoke the next morning. Frank and I were not comfortable with this arrangement, but Joe was an adult and we could only do so much.

CHAPTER 25

Joe's Last Days

The telephone rang about 3 A.M. Saturday morning and my heart felt as though it flew out of my body. Oh God, I thought. It's Joe, something is wrong!

Joe's pastor was on the telephone.

"Betty, I heard a terrible crash and when I came into Joe's room, he was on the floor and unable to move. He wants you to come right away and I have already called his doctor and Emergency Medical Service."

In the background, I could hear Joe's voice. He sounded terrified.

"Tell her to hurry, I can't move my right side. Tell her to hurry."

Frank and I arrived at the Rectory in less than 15 minutes. The entire time we were driving over to Nativity Rectory I kept praying, Oh God, don't let him be blind and paralyzed. Please God, take him before we ever get there, don't leave him blind and totally disabled and immobilized. How will he ever, ever manage?

When we arrived at Joe's house, the doctor and the EMS had already arrived and we only spoke for a few minutes before we all left for the hospital. While Joe was put through some tests, I ran back to Blessed Sacrament Church to 6:30 A.M. Mass. Father Hanley had special prayers for Joe's recovery. There were several members of Joe's parish in church, so I suppose the word got around that he was in hospital again.

I went back to the hospital emergency room and shortly after that, they took us up to the stroke unit. During this time, Joe was able to speak without any difficulty and he was very anxious to know what had happened. Neither one of us used the word stroke, but whatever Joe Maher was, he was no fool, and he knew exactly what had happened.

Shortly afterward, the doctors began to arrive. They all told me essentially the same thing. Joe had suffered a Brain Stem Stroke. The worst kind, and this could result in death within a matter of days. I spoke with the doctors and it was decided that we should have Frank phone Joe's brother and sister in Chicago and tell them they should try and fly to Charleston as soon as possible.

Joe grew weaker and weaker at a rather rapid pace. By that afternoon, many of Joe's friends and acquaintances had come to say their final good-byes. This procession of visitors continued all weekend. Since I knew how adamant Joe was about having no heroic measures taken to prolong his life, I was able to remind him over and over that he was not in intensive care but rather on a regular floor and that was why he was allowed so many visitors. He would try to answer that he understood, but by this time his speech was becoming very difficult to understand.

He must have been terrified, unable to see where he was and what was happening to him. Some people didn't understand why I insisted that so many visitors were allowed in the room, but I had taken care of Joe for four years and no one had asked what I was doing or how things were going with him. So in these last days of his life, I felt no obligation to explain anything to anyone. I knew that Joe would have supported me in this and I just continued to whisper to him, "Trust me, Joe, we are only making you comfortable. You know you are not in intensive care by the number of visitors."

Joe would blink his eyes, and I would beg God to be merciful, as I could not bear to think of his agony, locked in this shell that was his body, without sight, speech, or the ability to do more than blink his eyes. I prayed for God to take him as quickly as possible.

CHAPTER 26

Letting Go

On September 15th, the day before Joe died, his temperature began to rise and it was obvious that Joe was rapidly losing strength and his time in this world was quickly running out. By mid morning, as though God knew there was a closure to be made, the hospital room that had been filled with people was suddenly empty except for Joe and myself.

I knew that after years of friendship and our special relationship during the past four years, that this might be my last time alone with Joe. As I took the side rail down from the bed, wiped his face with a cold cloth, and talked to him about his illness, I hugged him and told him how important he was to me and my family and how much we loved him. I told him how blessed we were to be chosen to share his life these past four years.

He always referred to this as "destiny" and insisted that since our meeting in the early 1960s, this predetermined course was put into motion by a Higher Power.

I asked Joe if he would like me to sing to him and though it was a great effort, he blinked his eyes twice for no. I laughed and I know he laughed with me. I told him that he should leave the room because I intended to sing anyway.

I began to sing his favorite song, even though the effort was tearing me apart and my chest and throat felt as if they would explode. Finally, I asked him, "Joe, are you afraid?"

He blinked his eyes twice for no and tried to move his head. Then I asked, "if you are not afraid, then are you ready?"

Yes, he answered in the only way he was able, with his eyes.

"Well Joe, when I leave this evening, I want you to go to sleep and let go. Do you understand what I mean by that? When you go to sleep, I want you to let go."

He blinked his eyes once for yes and tried to say something to me.

"Joe, are you calling me your Irish Colleen?" He tried to nod and blinked his eyes.

"Are you telling me you love us?"

Again he blinked. And with that, he was lying on his left side and two huge tears rolled from his eyes.

"Joe, don't try to speak, we don't need words. My soul speaks to your soul and my heart speaks to your heart."

Again, he blinked showing me that he heard and understood everything I said. So once again I repeated, "Remember, Joe, when you go to sleep, I want you to let go and when you wake up we are all going to be together again. I'm ready for you to let go."

My voice began to break and I could tell that he knew I was upset.

"Let go, Joe, just let go for my sake and for your sake."

He blinked once and at that moment several people walked into the room. I suppose you might say that was the end of our personal closure. I stepped into the hall to thank God for those last hours and for the strength it took to speak to Joe about letting go. I think that my telling him this was a relief to him that the end was near. At this moment, Joe Maher did not fear death, he feared life.

Later that night after kissing Joe good-bye, Frank and I went to the nurses' station and spoke with the nurse taking care of Joe. We asked her opinion of his condition, and she said what I already knew. She felt that it would only be a matter of hours. I told her I had my closure and I would not be back that night but to call me when it was over. Otherwise I would return at 5 A.M. in the morning.

In the early hours of September 16th, we received the call that Joe had passed away.

We went over for one final good-bye. It was the end of a long friendship going back to the early 1960s. We had bowled together, and we had worked together at Blessed Sacrament School and Parish. Joe had been transferred into and out of the Charleston area but always when he was in town, he'd drop by and visit me at my work, saying, "Don't tell anyone I was in town." I would call him an egomaniac and ask who would care. This always made him laugh.

As a true follower of Jesus Christ, Joe has joined the Communion of Saints and now awaits the resurrection of the dead and life everlasting.

CHAPTER 27

What Will It Be Like At the End of My Life

If Joe could have written the final chapter of his life, I believe he would have said, "Lord, let it be quick." And it was-five days from the day he had the stroke until he passed away.

And he would have said, "Lord, don't let me suffer because as I suffer the people whom I love will suffer too." And when asked, he would deny all pain and discomfort and hopefully he was telling the truth.

He would have said, "Lord, give me loving and compassionate caregivers." And God knows that his doctors and all the hospital staff were wonderful to him and to us.

And finally, he would say, "Lord, let me be surrounded by the people I love and who love me in return." And God knows he was. Every day, the hospital room was filled with these friends and relatives, and he knew we were there and he felt our love.

CHAPTER 28

The Final Good-bye

We stood together, the four of us—Frank, my son Gary, my granddaughter Barbara, and myself. Our tears were competing with the downpour of rain, and we held one another close both for strength and warmth. I had my eyes closed and I heard a door slam a short distance to my right, then two doors closed directly in front of me. When I looked, the hearse was driving out of the parking area of the Church of the Nativity.

As though we had rehearsed our parts, four hands went up and four voices said "Bye, Joe, Bye."

"Please, God, let this be a terrible nightmare."

As I looked around the empty yard, I thought it might be a dream, but when Frank led me into the school hall, where they were holding the reception for family and friends, I knew that we had just said good-bye to one of the most compassionate, nonjudgmental, and undoubtedly most courageous priests ever to serve in the Diocese of Charleston. He was goodness personified, a true holy man with extraordinary humility and unswerving dedication. An inspiration to all who knew him.

Reverend Joseph Maher had begun the first step of his final journey back to Chicago, back to St. Boniface Cemetery to rest forever with his parents, his beloved sister , and his youngest brother.

God bless you, Joe, we love you!

CHAPTER 29

Life Goes On

And now Frank and I continue to go to the places that Joe loved. Every Friday night, we go to the Elks Lodge and sit with our friends. Before the evening is over, someone will say, "Gosh, I miss Joe," or "Gee, it's sad and lonely not having Joe to dance with."

I close my eyes and see Joe somewhere in heaven, dancing with angels and I smile and say, "Be a free spirit, Joe, we love and miss you with all of our hearts, but you be the free spirit you wanted to be these past five years."

I hear him say to the angels as he used to say to us, "I want to dance, I didn't come here to sit!"

His spirit lives on in our hearts.

Appendix I
Dedication

Father Maher dedicated this letter as a tribute to Frank and me, which would be given to us in the event of his death. In life, he thanked us a million times for assisting him during his last years. In death, he gives us the ultimate tribute, his eternal love.

I am now writing a very special note in reference to a very dear friend, Irish Colleen, and special angel-Betty White and her husband, Frank. They have given so much of themselves to assist me in my blindness. I do not know how to express my gratitude to Betty for all she has done for me and has given to me. By that, I mean helping to rebuild my confidence in myself. I honestly don't think I'd have accomplished what I have done without their assistance.

As I say, I have not mentioned any of this before, because I wanted to dedicate this particularly to them. I use the words: my Guardian Angel, my Irish Colleen or my Eyes in describing Betty. Her assistance in taking me out for walks, and feeding me meals and giving me laughter and joy, taking me out to various places of enjoyment made me feel like a real human being.

I know I am very limited in what I can do, but with Betty's assistance and her encouragement she has helped me so very much. Words can never be expressed from my heart the gratitude I feel for her help and assistance. Whenever I am in need, or whether I feel down and out, she was always there to help me and boost me up and make me laugh.

The bitterness I've felt in reference to (what is the word I want to use?)— so far as the Priesthood is concerned. I have felt so alone. The Brotherhood of the Priesthood for one who is blind simply is not there. The hours of loneliness— being by oneself hour after hour. But again, Betty helped me through these hours of loneliness by words of encouragement and strength.

In my moments of depression, in this bitterness which I deeply felt, Betty was there with words of encouragement, never letting me take things for granted. With her laughter and her nagging and her determination that I could do things, she assisted me in so many, many ways. Never letting me give up when so many times I did want to simply be left alone and I wanted to give up, I wanted to die! But with her support, encouragement, and strength, she enabled me to be where I am today. I know I have a long road to go to accomplish—I pray someday—full control of my life. And this is the greatest difficulty, not having control of one's own life, but having to depend on others for everything.

And so it is with Betty's help and guidance and her eternal nagging that she has made me carry on. I am now able to assist at Nativity church and I wait and see what the future holds for me. And now Betty and Frank, when you read this, I thank you. I thank you from the bottom of my heart.

Smile, laugh, sing. You two are just two beautiful and lovely people, and please forgive me for indeed you two have been my dear pal and my guardian angel/Irish Colleen. I love you with all of my heart.

Appendix 2

Rev. John Dunne, SMA Superior, African Foundation Loma Toga, Africa

For some 20 years, Frank and I have known Fr. John Dunne to be one of our dearest friends. We met Fr. John when he was doing graduate studies at Boston College in Boston, Massachusetts. We have been very fortunate to be able to visit with him occasionally when he would visit the United States or when we were visiting Ireland.

We planned to visit Ireland in the summer of 1996, called Fr. John, and were delighted to hear that he was on vacation and would be delighted to join us for a portion of our tour around the countryside. Fr. John met us at the airport in Shannon, Ireland and was a little surprised to find that we had an extra traveler, Father Joe Maher.

The following is a tribute to Father Maher written at my request by Fr. Dunne:

People come into our lives in the most unusual ways. This is a truism but there is always a truth hidden in our truisms. The important truth for me of how someone like Fr Joe came in to my life is that it happened so simply and without knowing it was taking place. But as this happened I became aware of the many different dimensions of the gift of sight and the loss of same. Can we ever be grateful enough for what we have received, and can we ever accept fully the loss of any one of the gifts given?

We met in Ireland in the summer of 1996. Father Joe was introduced as a friend who decided to visit Ireland with Betty and Frank. No mention was made of physical limitations, but I gradually became aware that Father Joe did not see too well or perhaps not at all.

In a very short time, I noticed the ease in which Father Joe was given coffee, and included in all discussions of rental car and travel route. It was obvious that he was to be an active member of our party.

As we traveled, I was able to see a side of Father Joe that was to be a regular feature of our time together. His presence and his acceptance of what was going on around him was evident but not easily put into words. He must have developed this over time since the beginning of his blindness. He now sat and had to accept being led by others and in my case, a stranger. Where to put one's trust in such circumstances.

We stopped at the beauty spots and took the usual photographs. At each viewing spot there was a clear and detailed account of what the scenery was like. A little about colors and landscape was presented by Betty to give Father Joe a feel of the place.

We visited craft shops, encouraged Fr. Joe to buy the souvenirs we liked and he smiled but did not bite saying, "I may be blind, but I am not stupid."

I stayed in the same room with Fr. Joe in the Bed and Breakfasts and then I really began to realize what it meant to be blind. How to find one's way around each new bedroom as the days rolled by is not easy if you cannot see. He did the tour with Betty, then had a supervised run and was finally on his own. I used to say, "Now, Joe, if you need any help, do ask and I will be happy to oblige."

However, Fr. Joe was determined to do it on his own.

He would visit the bathroom during the night and of course make the trip on his own. But at what price! He would begin by establishing his bearings from his bed. From there, he would walk into things, then after a short pause, begin again; and he would hit his head against things. He would swear quietly and then carry on with determination and courage. He never asked for help. I would say, "Are you alright, Joe?"

and he would invariable say, "Yes, I am fine."

Call it what you like, independence, stubbornness, or shear will power, it was something that evoked strange sentiments in me-anger at the plight of Joe, laughter at his swearing, or the surprise crash sound when he walked into something he did not expect, frustration at not being able to help without intrusion, wonder at what was going on in his heart and mind.

For Fr. Joe it was all just a part of his wonderful vacation. He loved and trusted the people around him, the visit went smoothly as he was loved and readily accepted by all.

Physical blindness is a very tangible and very real. There is a blindness that is more frightening than the loss of physical sight. In our world of instant this and that, there is an incessant need to know and to have clarity. We are blinded sometimes by this need. It reminds us of the fear we have of entering into the unknown, a fear of the insecure darkness. This is expressed by a fear or reluctance to enter into relationships of marriage or other vocational choices.

We do not risk very much; we need to know beforehand; we must have clarity; we cannot accept that life is a journey in which we struggle step by step to remove ourselves from protective vulnerability. We can only do this by entering into the darkness of our lives at any given time.

Blindness invites us to choose between dependence and independence. It offers us the gift of receptivity, to be led by others or the Spirit, as opposed to selectivity, where we choose and try to control all that happens. God's will is no longer simply what happens to me. It is rather an adventure that I am invited to undertake.

Fr. Joe, in the short time I knew you there was something of the nature of this discovery for myself. I do not know how your journey was and it is not necessary for me to have the details. I am sure though that our meeting was important for me. I thank you for just being Joe in all the different ways I knew you in Ireland. Now you see clearly; and there is no need for lamplight or sunlight anymore! Can you help keep us in the light?

To Betty and Frank a word of thanks for introducing me to Fr Joe. A real surprise and a joy! Thanks for the wonderful friendship you had with Joe and for the love, courage, understanding, strength and kindness you showed with him and in turn evoked in the good priest himself. We can celebrate that during our time of traveling together.

Appendix 3

A TRIBUTE TO JOE MAHER

Charles "Buddy" Sirisky—Esteemed Leading Knight
To Our Absent Brother

My Brothers,

It is with the utmost respect and admiration that special recognition be given our departed Brother Revered Father Joseph G. Maher who passed away September 16, 1998.

Joe was initiated in 1997, I remember him well. As Esquire, I provided an escort due to his being blind. Joe had recently retired from active priesthood in the Charleston Catholic Diocese and was Pastor of the Church of the Nativity on James Island for many years. He was ordained a priest in 1955.

Joe's dear friends, Frank and Betty White, introduced him to their Elks family, after first hearing the Eleven O'clock Toast he was very touched and committed to membership in our Lodge. Joe and the Whites were regulars at most functions and faithful to the Friday Night gatherings.

Joe loved the dancing and talking with old friends and endeared many new friends. He was so happy with his newfound Elks family.

The last time I saw Joe he was at the Labor Day picnic. He suffered a stroke and passed away September 16. He was 71 years old. I asked him if he would deliver the Homily for the Memorial Service in December, he respectfully declined because of his physical limitations.

Joe's love of Elkdom was culminated by an Elks Memorial Service in his honor by the officers of the Lodge. The Service was held at the Church of the Nativity on James Island.

It is therefore fitting to conclude this tribute from the Station of Brotherly love: "It has smiles and laughter for us in seasons of Joy and it sits with us in the hour of bereavement. It teaches us to scatter flowers along life's pathway and to speak words of kindness to the living as well as to cherish the memory of the dead."

Appendix 4

Memories of Father Joe Maher
Inez Germroth

I met Father Joseph Maher in 1965 when I first moved to Charleston He was Associate Pastor and disciplinarian of the school at Blessed Sacrament Parish. He baptized my youngest child. My older children attended Blessed Sacrament school and I felt at that time, this was a true, compassionate, and holy priest.

As a young mother at 30 with 6 children, I found him truly understanding with the problems of a young, large family.

Our family moved to James Island in 1967 and attended the Church of the Nativity. For the next 20 years, I only saw Father Maher periodically as he was assigned to other parishes in South Carolina.

In 1985, a few months after my husband's death in April, he was assigned to Nativity parish. He became my counselor, my pastor, and friend. After working with Father Maher on different commissions, he asked me to become a Eucharistic minister so I could take communion to the shut-ins.

I told Father Maher I wasn't worthy and good enough to do this. He laughed and said, "Inez, we are none worthy, but God needs our help and we are good enough." After 5 o'clock Mass one day, he asked me to wait in the church. He talked, prayed with me, and commissioned me as a Eucharistic minister.

A few years later, he was transferred to St. Anthony's in Walterboro, South Carolina. He did not forget his former parishioners. Several times he called me and asked me to visit and take communion to one of his former parishioners.

After his blindness and recovery from hospital stays and a rest period in Chicago with his family, he was welcomed back to Nativity parish as Priest-in-Residence. He was a very brave, courageous man the way he handled his blindness, but he would always say to me, "Inez, you don't know."

I never thought that I would be driving Father Maher to do his priestly duties. Every Monday at 2:45 P.M., I would pick him up and take him to visit the shut-ins. I'll never forget the smiles and happiness on their faces when he would visit. He always left them with a smile. They enjoyed the visits so much. He was truly a blessing to them.

During our drives, we talked and confided in each other. We shared a lot of laughter and tears. He would say to me, "Inez, keep your faith-I've lost mine." Then we would have a big laugh and he would say, "God bless you."

Sister Noreen called me with the news that Father Joe had suffered a stroke. It brought back our last visits two weeks prior. He had postponed our visits for a week because he was having minor surgery. He tried to assure me on our last visit that this surgery was minor and to please not worry. The next time I saw him he was in the hospital after having a stroke. He would let me know that he knew I was there by squeezing my hand and blinking his eyes for yes or no.

The illness, the wake, and the funeral all seem like a dream. It's hard to believe he is gone.

I will not say, "Good-bye," I'll just say, "So long" until we meet again.

To know Father Joe was to love him.